PERSECUTED
BUT NOT
FORSAKEN

DR. LOVAN SANDS

HOV
PUBLISHING

Persecuted But Not Forsaken

HOV Publishing a division of HOV, LLC.
www.90daybookcreation.com
hopeofvision@gmail.com

Front Cover Design by Hope of Vision Designs
Inside layout by Hope of Vision Designs
Editor/Proofread: HOV Publishing Editorial Team

Contact the Author, Dr. Lovan Sands at lovan.sands@gmail.com

For further information regarding special discounts on bulk purchases, please visit www.90daybookcreation.com

ISBN Paperback: 978-1-955107-37-2
ISBN eBook: 978-1-955107-36-5

Printed in the United States of America

Dedication

I dedicate this book with heartfelt gratitude to my beloved mother, Pauline Porter. Your unwavering support and encouragement have been a beacon of strength, reminding me that I can conquer all things through Christ who strengthens me.

To my son, Pastor Maurice Humber, your steadfast presence and assistance have been invaluable in bringing this book to fruition. Your support has been a constant source of motivation.

To my dear friend and covenant sister, Dr. Von Brand, your prayers and encouragement have uplifted me throughout this journey. Your unwavering support has been a blessing.

Last but certainly not least, to my husband, Apostle

Elvin Sands, your belief in me, even during moments of self-doubt, has been a guiding light. Thank you for embracing and supporting me in fulfilling God's calling on my life. Your love and encouragement mean everything to me.

Introduction

As a child, I always felt like I stood apart from others. I never quite fit in and was frequently misunderstood. Growing up in a household with six siblings, I found myself being the outspoken one, always ready to stand up for what I believed was right, even when it meant facing persecution and disapproval. Writing became my comfort during those times of turmoil; whenever something felt wrong, I would pour my thoughts onto paper, finding comfort and clarity through my words.

I always liked religious education in school, not realizing at the time, now feels like a part of a larger plan. Looking back, I realize that from a young age, I was being guided by a higher purpose. However, my early school years were not without their challenges. I remember a particular classmate who would become angry if I didn't engage in playtime with him. One day, his frustration turned violent, and he stabbed me in the hand with his pencil. It was a painful experience, both physically and emotionally, and it left me with a silent hurt growing inside me.

My daddy was very strict, and it cast a shadow over my childhood. He demanded perfection, instilling a fear that ran deep. Being late for school or failing an exam was simply unacceptable in our household. Anything less than an A would result in his severe discipline, often resulting in bruises that colored our skin black and blue. My father was not one to be questioned or challenged, not even by my mother, leaving me feeling isolated and without anyone to confide in during those difficult times.

I pray that if you are reading this book, and you are going through what I went through as a child, you will seek help. As a child, I couldn't talk about my pain without facing punishment. We didn't have the privileges that other children enjoyed. We didn't have cellphones back then, only limited television time between certain times and then I had to be in my room studying. Feeling hurt and rejected, I had no one to confide in. Sometimes I would sit in the classroom while the teacher was teaching and all I could think about was the memories of the beatings. I could not tell my teacher, afraid that she may call my parents and my dad shows up at the school. This will cause further beatings from my father. When the belt wasn't strong enough to beat us, dad had a friend that is a mechanic, and he would give my dad a belt he cut from a car tire so he could beat us.

As a child, I struggled severely with asthma. My condition was so bad I thought I was going to die after seeing all the good doctors in town. It only got worse. My mom sought healing for me, taking me to countless conferences and church services in our town, where fervent prayers were offered on my behalf. Despite all our efforts, the asthma persisted, leaving me fearing for my life. It was a debilitating condition, restricting me from enjoying simple pleasures like eating rice or having a cold drink. I was even confined indoors during colder times. However, as I got older and began to believe God's promises for myself, I witnessed a remarkable transformation. Through faith and perseverance, the asthma gradually disappeared.

I'm grateful that despite the challenges, I completed my education and started working. Eventually, I went back to school to study Cosmetology and later opened my own beauty salon. The difficulties I faced in my childhood did not define my future; instead, they fueled my determination to succeed.

Encountering some hurtful relationships proved to be a painful journey with the wrong partners. Now I realize that in my search for love, I often look for it in the wrong places, resulting in frequent heartaches. Growing up was not easy; my mother's unwavering commitment to her church meant our family spent much of our time in church also. Childhood friendships and going out were not allowed, it was a rough upbringing because my dad enforced strict rules then, as he does to this day.

Preface

In the journey of faith, we often find ourselves facing persecution and trials that seem bewildering at first. It's not until we grow in our spiritual maturity that we can look back and understand how these experiences were orchestrated by God to lead us to our intended destination.

Scripture reminds us in 2 Corinthians 4:8-10 that though we may be troubled and persecuted, we are never forsaken or destroyed. Even when we face internal fears and external conflicts, we are upheld by the power of Christ's resurrection, demonstrating His grace in our lives.

Throughout my own walk, I've encountered challenges, particularly within the church community. Despite faithfully carrying out my assignments, I faced persecution and slander. It was a painful realization that those I trusted could turn against me. Yet, through it all, I stood firm, trusting in God's vindication.

Mistakes were made along the way, especially in the choices I made and the connections I formed. Jealousy and betrayal lurked even among those closest to me. Yet, God remained faithful, sustaining me through every trial and revealing His truth in the face of falsehood.

It's crucial to remember that our journey may be fraught with opposition, but it's in these moments that our faith is tested and strengthened. As Nehemiah declared in Nehemiah 6:3, we must remain steadfast in our work, refusing to be distracted or deterred by the schemes of the enemy.

In Psalm 24:4-5, we are reminded of the necessity of purity and integrity in our walk with God. Despite the trials and tribulations we face, our hands must remain clean, and our hearts pure, reflecting our unwavering trust in the Lord.

Ultimately, we must surrender our battles to God,

trusting Him to fight on our behalf. Though we may face attacks on our character and integrity, we can take comfort in knowing that God will always uphold His truth and protect His servants. As we navigate the challenges of this journey, let us cling to the assurance of who we are in God and remain steadfast in His Word.

Contents

Chapter 1

You Had to Go Through It

In our Christian journey, we often encounter seasons of trial and tribulation, where the path ahead seems unclear. It's during these times that we may struggle to understand the purpose behind our struggles. Yet, in the confusion, I've learned that God remains faithfully by our side, ready to lead, guide, and direct us—if only we let Him. We must always remind ourselves of God's promises, anchoring our faith in His Word.

Psalm 139:7-10 beautifully illustrates this truth: "Whither shall I go from thy spirit? or whither shall I flee from thy presence? If I ascend up into heaven, thou art there:

if I make my bed in hell, behold, thou art there. If I take the wings of the morning, and dwell in the uttermost parts of the sea; Even there shall thy hand lead me, and thy right hand shall hold me."

David's reflection reminds us that God's omnipresence knows no bounds; He is with us in every circumstance, whether in moments of joy or despair. God is everywhere.

Indeed, God orchestrates every aspect of our lives with a divine plan and purpose. Though we may not always understand the reasons behind our trials, we can trust that God is working all things for our good. Yet, this assurance doesn't exempt us from the necessity of enduring through the process. As the saying goes, Trouble don't last always. If God leads us to a challenge, He will undoubtedly see us through it.

When faced with circumstances beyond our control, it's tempting to rely on our own strength to fix things. However, the key is to surrender our burdens to God in prayer, releasing our worries and concerns into His capable hands. Rather than complaining about our situation, let us position ourselves in prayer, acknowledging God's sovereignty and seeking His guidance.

So, when life throws its inevitable curveballs, remember to relinquish control, place your trust in God, and allow His presence to guide you through every trial and tribulation.

Chapter 2

Take Your Hands Off It

I remember many days when I would try to figure out how to pay my bills, and my attempts to find solutions only seemed to bring about fear and doubt, especially during the chaos of the pandemic. But one day, the Lord spoke to my spirit saying, take your hands off it, "I didn't bring you this far to leave you," His voice resonated within me, and I shifted my focus. It was a turning point when I allowed God to take the lead.

As I shifted my focus from my own understanding to unwavering trust in God, I witnessed never before manifestations of His power. It became clear that God desires for us to lean and depend on Him. It was a lesson learned through faith, a realization that sometimes challenges arise not to break us but to strengthen our faith and deepen our trust in God's unfailing promises.

Proverbs 3:5-6 says: "Trust in the Lord with all thine heart; and lean not unto thine own understanding. In all thy ways acknowledge him, and he shall direct thy paths." These verses serve as a roadmap for navigating life's uncertainties, urging us to place our trust wholeheartedly in God's guidance and provision.

To experience God's move in our lives, we must surrender ourselves fully to His will and acknowledge His sovereignty. As believers we must allow God to take his rightful place in our life. We cannot say we are serving Him, and our heart is far from Him. We cannot say, we are serving Him, and we only pray and show up to church when we are in need of a breakthrough and once we get our breakthrough, we stop praying and going to church. God is looking for accountability. He is looking for people to serve him in spirit and truth. The Bible says in 3 John 1:2. "Beloved, I wish above all things that thou mayest prosper and be in health, even as thy soul prospereth." God wants to prosper us, but we must trust Him.

The temptation to take matters into our own hands will only serve to disqualify us from the blessings God has in store. Remember, trouble is temporary, subject to change by the hand of a God whose power knows no boundaries.

It is important to know ourselves in our identity in Christ. Because if we don't know who we are in Him, we will be defined by who they say we are, and we will never live in who God says we are. The enemy will attack our minds with doubts and confusion, but we must remain steadfast, tuning our spirits to the voice of God. Only then can we truly embrace the promises and purposes He has ordained for our lives, undeterred by the plans of the enemy.

Chapter 3
Dealing With Rejection

At some point in life, everyone faces rejection—it's an inevitable part of our journey. When someone you deeply care about rejects you, the pain can feel like a sharp stab to the heart. It's excruciating, and in the midst of it, it seems like the ache will never fade. Yet, confronting and processing this rejection is essential for growth and change. We've all experienced these moments, and some of us try to escape the harsh reality of rejection. But these attempts only provide temporary relief, never truly addressing the root issue. Recognizing rejection as a spiritual battle is crucial for finding deliverance from its grip.

When rejection takes hold, it distorts our perception of reality. We become easily offended to criticism and suspicious of those around us. Yet, the key to overcoming rejection lies in surrendering to God's will. By releasing our grip on bitterness and resentment, we allow God to work in our lives and shape our identity. Refusing to let rejection dictate our worth is essential for reclaiming our sense of self.

Even within the church community, rejection can manifest when individuals face disappointment or disagreement. Rather than addressing the underlying issue, some may simply flee to another congregation. However, until the spirit of rejection is confronted and dealt with, it will continue to poison our relationships and hinder our growth. Recognizing rejection's toxic grip is the first step toward liberation and healing.

Never allow one person's opinion or a single incident to define your worth. Your value should never hinge on the perceptions of others. Just because someone holds a certain view of you doesn't mean it reflects the truth. As Psalm 27:10 assures us, "When my father and my mother forsake me, then the Lord will take me up." It's vital to remember that you are not alone in facing rejection.

I've observed individuals clinging to connections that God has severed because they are still grappling with feelings of rejection and the desire to be accepted. But it's essential to surrender to God's plan and allow Him to work in our lives. Jeremiah 29:11 says, "For I know the thoughts that I think toward you, saith the Lord, thoughts of peace, and not of evil, to give you an expected end." Trusting in His plan ensures that we'll reach the expected end He has in store for us.

Chapter 4

When The Wrong People Leave Your Life Good Things Begin to Happen

In this journey of faith, learning is constant. I've learned firsthand about the impact of being connected to the wrong people—it can act as a spiritual roadblock. My husband and I experienced this when we were involved with a religious organization. Initially, everything seemed fine, but after four months, I noticed a downturn in my business. It felt like there were obstacles everywhere until I sought God through fasting and prayer. His guidance led us to shift, and upon doing so, we witnessed a release of the blockages and received even greater blessings.

Trusting in the Lord's leading, rather than our emotions, is crucial. Sometimes, He orchestrates divine connections, directly leading us to what we need. It's essential to evaluate our inner circle because oftentimes, our adversaries are those closest to us, disguised as friends. We must not judge solely by appearances.

As John 10:27-28 teaches, "My sheep hear my voice, and I know them, and they follow me: And I give unto them eternal life; and they shall never perish, neither shall any man pluck them out of my hand."

Staying within the will of God is paramount; follow His voice and desire what He wants for you. When God instructs you to shift, it's crucial to heed His guidance. Jeremiah 29:11 says. "For I know the thoughts that I think toward you, saith the Lord, thoughts of peace, and not of evil, to give you an expected end." This scripture reassures us of God's plans for our well-being, not for harm, to grant us a hopeful future.

Holding on to the wrong relationships can rob you of your peace. Investing in individuals who don't genuinely have your best interests at heart leads to confusion, as Matthew 7:6 warns against, "Give not that which is holy unto the dogs, neither cast ye your pearls before swine, lest they trample them under their feet, and turn again and rend you." Just as pigs would trample pearls, some people fail to appreciate your worth. Despite your efforts, they may never recognize the God within you. In such cases, it's wise to distance yourself from those who merely tolerated you in the past. It's time to step into a season where you are celebrated rather than just tolerated.

Chapter 5

Unlocking Unforgiveness

Holding onto unforgiveness is like drinking poison; it harms you more than anyone else. I've experienced this firsthand, particularly when faced with false accusations that tarnished my reputation. The weight of unforgiveness manifested physically, causing stomach tightness and migraines. However, when I obediently forgave those who wronged me, I felt a shift. Despite the initial challenge, I heard the Lord's voice urging me to forgive, and as I complied, I began to feel an outpouring of love and compassion. Additionally, I realized the importance of forgiving myself; often, we indulge in self-destructive emotional patterns that lack God's presence. Rather than directing anger towards the individual, it's crucial to recognize the spiritual forces at play and address them accordingly.

Ephesians 6:12 says, "For we wrestle not against flesh and blood, but against principalities, against powers, against the rulers of the darkness of this world, against spiritual wickedness in high places." Unforgiveness breeds bitterness rather than fostering growth; it's a stronghold of principality. On this Christian journey, it's essential to discern beyond people's outward demeanor and recognize the spirits they harbor. By doing so, we can spare ourselves from unnecessary pain and turmoil. Pay attention not only to words but also to the spirit behind them, for as Luke 6:45 reveals, "A good man out of the good treasure of his heart bringeth forth that which is good; and an evil man out of the evil treasure of his heart bringeth forth that which is evil: for of the abundance of the heart his mouth speaketh."

Therefore, in addressing hurt and unforgiveness, whether within marriage, family, friendships, or workplaces, it's vital to release them. Remember, forgiveness isn't solely for the benefit of others but primarily for your own liberation and peace. Embrace deliverance and freedom in the name of Jesus.

Chapter 6

Don't Quit

Winners never quit; perseverance is key as you run this race, knowing that you will finish strong. Without a plan, your aspirations may fail; therefore, diligently pursue your goals. Your visions and ideas will bear fruit only when you take proactive steps towards them. Remember, your story is still being written.

Failure only has the final say if you allow it. Our God is capable of turning our setbacks and mistakes into opportunities to glorify His name. Consider Jeremiah, the weeping prophet, chosen during a dire period for Israel. Initially hesitant due to his youth and perceived inadequacies,

God addressed his fears directly. He instructed Jeremiah not to doubt his abilities but to trust in God's provision. Similarly, in moments of doubt and despair, we can find strength by placing our trust in God's plan.

During the pandemic, among the global spread of the virus, it's crucial to remain steadfast in your faith. Trust in God's protection and provision for His children. Position yourself to align with God's purpose for your life, disregarding the opinions and criticisms of others. Avoid negativity, as it can lead to doubt and despair. Surround yourself with positive influences—individuals who inspire and uplift you—while distancing yourself from those who engage in idle gossip and negativity. Choose your inner circle wisely, connecting with those who recognize your value and encourage you to pursue greatness. Seek out mentors and allies who have already achieved what you aspire to attain. Together, let us press onward towards the fulfillment of our divine destinies.

Chapter 7

Don't Give the Enemy A Seat
At Your Table

When you're called to greatness, it's crucial to keep your focus on the path ahead. Obstacles, even in the form of people influenced by the enemy, may try to block your journey. But, when you heed God's guidance, you'll never stray from the right path.

When my husband and I embarked on our ministry journey, we faced opposition, even from leaders who questioned our calling. Ironically, these were the same individuals who once faced similar challenges in their own ministries. However, as they ascended in their positions, they seemed to forget their humble beginnings and began to judge us with pride. Despite their doubts, we remained steadfast in the confidence of God's calling upon our lives.

I can remember a female Apostle casting doubt upon our ministry, suggesting that I lacked the ability to go international. Her words stung, and for a moment, I almost gave up on my assignment. It was during this time of doubt that we sought counsel from the late Apostle Rodney Roberts, a seasoned Apostolic father now resting with the Lord. His prayers and prophetic words reassured us, affirming that we carried an Apostolic sound within us.

With us being new to ministry, the criticism could have damaged us emotionally and spiritually, but I refused to let it define me. Instead, I turned to the Lord for strength and began to encourage myself in Him. Remember, never allow the words of others to define your identity in God.

There have been nights when tears were my only relief, as church hurt weighed heavily upon my heart. In those moments, I had to remind myself of who God said I am in His kingdom. It's confusing how some of the very leaders who once spoke into our lives concerning our ministry are now the ones casting doubt upon our calling. Accusations flew – I was labeled a witch, while my husband was branded a warlock. We've walked into rooms where the expressions from some of the same leaders looked like we had leprosy. But we refused to be intimidated by them. Despite the trials, we held onto God's promises and remained steadfast in our assignments.

Understanding your identity in the kingdom and discerning God's calling upon your life is paramount. With the imminent return of Christ, it's crucial not to linger in the wrong places or among the wrong company. Shift your focus away from the past, for there are some who will never embrace your gifts and calling. But, rest assured, God remains sovereign over your destiny.

As David did in 1 Samuel 30:6, by encouraging himself in the Lord his God. Sometimes it's the people you trust the most that want to destroy you. God wants to do remarkable things in your life and ministry. Stay focused, and don't allow the enemy a seat at your table.

Instead of finding security, we often find ourselves consumed by paranoia. Instead of growing in confidence, fear begins to cripple us, threatening to overshadow our faith. Never allow your fears to drown out your faith, for that is where the enemy seeks to dismantle the vision God has bestowed upon you. When fear takes hold, doubts about God's plan can arise, as the adversary's voice grows louder than your faith.

Despite what people may have said about my husband and I, predicting our relationship would not last, we've defied the odds and remained together through the years. It's essential to believe in yourself, to possess unwavering confidence in the promises God has spoken over your life. As 1 John 4:4 reminds us, "Greater is he that is in you, than he that is in the world." Embrace the greatness within you, living out the identity God has ordained for you, regardless of the negativity spoken by your enemies.

Chapter 8

The Pain and The Process

My journey was very painful, and I thought that God had forgotten me. It's in those moments that it seems like our prayers are unheard, as if God has turned a deaf ear to our cries. But I've come to realize that during our trials, God often remains silent, much like a teacher in a classroom during an exam. It's a period of testing, and His silence doesn't indicate His absence.

Remember, when you feel like you've hit rock bottom, God is up to something marvelous behind the scenes. Just as Job, he didn't understand why he had to go through and endured such loss, we too may find ourselves stripped of the very things we hold close to us. Job's story, found in Job 1:12, "And the Lord said unto Satan, Behold, all that he hath is in thy power; only upon himself put not forth thine hand. So Satan went forth from the presence of the Lord." The scripture Illustrates how God allowed Satan to test him, granting permission for affliction to enter his life. What do you do when the permission is given by God to Satan?

Could it be the things that you lost, God gave Satan permission to take it because you were too distracted by it! Sometimes, the distractions we hold on to must be removed for us to fully grasp God's purpose for our lives. Throughout Job's ordeal, his friends added to his suffering by falsely accusing him of sinning against God. It's in such times of testing that true friendships are revealed.

In the midst of your process, be discerning about your connections. Don't give up, even when the journey becomes painful. Embrace the pain, for it is molding you for your divine purpose. Remember, true peace is found in the presence of God, where Job eventually found comfort.

Despite his immense suffering, Job's story didn't end in despair. In Job 42:12, "So the Lord blessed the latter end of Job more than his beginning: for he had fourteen thousand sheep, and six thousand camels, and a thousand yoke of oxen, and a thousand she asses." We see how God restored him abundantly, blessing him with even greater prosperity than before. Your comeback will always be greater and victorious if you stick to the process.

Chapter 9

Stop Doubting God

In our daily journey with God, it's crucial to understand our identity in Him. Life's challenges may come unexpectedly, but it's up to us to turn those sour lemons into sweet lemonade and keep pressing forward on this Christian path. There will be days when doubts creep in, and you may even feel abandoned by God. But remember, just like a teacher quiets the classroom during a test, God may seem silent during your trials.

Keep in mind that victory in this race of life isn't reserved for the fastest, but for those who persist until the end. Speak words of life over yourself, even in the midst of adversity, for champions never give up. No matter what you face, never waver in your trust in God's promises; He will always fulfill His word in His perfect timing.

Chapter 10

God Can

Sometimes the word that God has spoken to you may not align with your current circumstances, but rest assured, He will fulfill it. As Numbers 23:19 reminds us, God is not a man that He should lie; if He has spoken, He will surely bring it to pass. God specializes in difficult situations, using them to showcase His glory.

Manifestations of God's promises often require our active participation. For instance, I always envisioned myself writing books, but it wasn't until I picked up the pen and started writing that I saw God bringing it to fruition. When God releases a word to you, take action and walk in obedience to His will. The late DR. MYLES MUNROE ENCOURAGED US TO "DIE EMPTY," emphasizing the importance of fulfilling our God-given assignments on Earth to honor Him.

Even when facing challenges, continue to pray God's word and maintain faith, knowing that if God brings you to it, He will bring you through it. Sometimes, those you expect to support you may become adversaries. God may orchestrate separation before promotion, even if it causes temporary pain, for He hears conversations we do not.

In this season of reset, release everything to God, as clinging to things may hinder your progress. Allow God to take center stage in your life and trust His perfect work within you. Remember, what He does is always well done.

Chapter 11

The Sting of Betrayal

Matthew 26:14-16 says, "Then one of the twelve, called Judas Iscariot, went unto the chief priests, And said unto them, What will ye give me, and I will deliver him unto you? And they covenanted with him for thirty pieces of silver. And from that time he sought opportunity to betray him."

Jesus experienced betrayal from one of His closest disciples, Judas Iscariot, who spent years with Him witnessing His miracles (raised the dead, sight to the blind, and the lame to walk) and teachings. Yes, this same Judas, chosen by Jesus and intimately known by Him, ultimately betrayed the one who not only loved him but also offered him the extraordinary privilege of walking and conversing personally with God. Despite being chosen as one of His followers, Judas succumbed to deception in his heart and mind, orchestrated by Satan, and betrayed Jesus for thirty pieces of silver. This act led to Judas's realization of his betrayal of an innocent man, prompting his tragic end by hanging himself. Those who betray you will eventually face their own consequences and live to regret their actions.

Becoming a Christian has opened my eyes in many ways; I've learned that sometimes your greatest adversaries may be seated right beside you in church or even other organizations. I've endured being lied about, persecuted, mocked, betrayed, scorned, laughed at, and called everything except a Child of God, all within the confines of the church. Despite the pain, I've used these experiences as fuel to motivate me.

Growing in my faith, I've come to understand that such trials are part of the process; even Jesus endured similar challenges. Some of those who once laughed in my face and even supported me became my greatest adversaries when God began to elevate my life and use me in ministry. They exemplified the spirit of Judas, consumed by jealousy and resentment. It's essential to beware of this "Judas spirit," where people bless you outwardly but speak ill of you behind your back. Some individuals will only tolerate you as long as you remain on their level, and if you allow it, they will exploit you. We often enable others to mistreat us due to what we represent. It's crucial to recognize your worth and understand who God has called you to be; only then will you truly appreciate yourself.

God will not permit you to be just tolerated; He intends for you to be celebrated. I've witnessed people sow into my life, only to criticize me when God begins to elevate me. I'm thankful for God's grace and mercy; He is indeed a faithful guardian. Remember, allowing the spirit of Judas to affect your character is unwise; remain discerning.

In 2 Timothy 2:12, it is written, "If we suffer, we shall also reign with him: if we deny him, he also will deny us:" Remember, your reward for enduring suffering will be great, so stand tall in the face of adversity. Never allow betrayal to embitter you; instead, always strive to forgive and move forward.

Bitterness is a common result of hurt that lingers in our hearts instead of being forgiven. It acts like weeds in a garden, gradually overtaking our hearts. We hold onto bitterness because we feel powerless to overcome it, allowing it to grow and constantly remind us of our past hurts. The danger lies in how bitterness can transform into anger and even uncontrolled wrath. It slowly poisons our hearts until we lose all joy. Therefore, it's crucial to address and release bitterness, replacing it with forgiveness and healing.

Chapter 12

Your Destiny Will Not Be Aborted

When God appoints and anoints you, your feelings or thoughts become insignificant; His word will prevail. Before my husband and I embarked on our pastoral journey, there were moments when I felt abandoned by God, despite the multitude of prophetic words spoken over our lives. We endured seasons marked by rejection, deceit, and betrayal, though we couldn't comprehend it then, it was all part of God's grand plan for our benefit.

Reflecting on 1 Samuel 16, we find David, a humble shepherd boy in the fields, chosen by God through the prophet Samuel to be the future king of Israel. Although Samuel initially assumed that Jesse's eldest son would be the chosen one, God's selection defied human expectations. David, the youngest and not as handsome as his brothers, was anointed by God for a significant purpose. It was a reminder that God does not judge based on outward appearances but on the purity of the heart.

See, David was anointed, appointed, chosen, and set apart by God. Despite not having the same outward appearance as his brothers, he was the one chosen for greatness. Along life's journey, disappointments will inevitably arise, but you mustn't give up. Remember, the only one who can stop you is yourself. Just as David had to wait on the Lord and go through a process despite being anointed as king, you too must go through your preparation season. Trust that it will all work together for your good. Even when you feel like you're failing, remain faithful to what God has called you to do. Sometimes, when God is elevating you, nothing around you will make sense because you've already outgrown that season.

Chapter 13

Never Allow Negativity to Keep You From Moving Forward

When the Lord called my husband and I to start our ministry, I struggled with confidence in myself and in who God called me to be. I found myself operating in the spirit of fear, worrying about what other leaders and people would say. I even used to hide the tattoos on my hand. But one day, the Lord rebuked me, saying that my witness would not be true if I hid my testimony and didn't embrace my true self. That rebuke gave me the boldness I needed to push forward in ministry and do what He called me to do.

My mother has been a great support in my life and

ministry. She always told me, "My daughter, whether you do good or bad, people will talk and criticize you. So continue to do good and always do what God calls you to do." With determination, faith, and courage, I started ministry. Despite facing persecution, I never felt forsaken by God because I had resolved to live and die for Him. Though things may not always go as we want, when God is in the vessel, we can ride out the storm.

In ministry, sometimes the very people you pray for are the ones who turn their backs on you. You must learn to release those who hurt you, forgive them, and move on. Another important lesson is to learn to encourage yourself in the Lord. Weeping may endure for a night, but joy comes in the morning.

Chapter 14

Wait On The Lord

To all my single ladies out there, I want to encourage you to wait on the Lord and stop making the wrong choices concerning relationships. When I look around the church, I see so many hurting women, and the majority of their pain stems from relationships. As long as you continue to do things your way, you will always end up in the wrong friendships or relationships. Jumping from one relationship to another will not help you; instead, give yourself time to heal. Be sold out to God and get busy with your assignment.

I can vividly recall my time in the world, partying, drinking, and going from one relationship to another. Nothing seemed to work until I got saved and came to Jesus. In fact, the so-called relationship I was in before I got saved took a dangerous turn when the man I was with attacked me. He hit me over the head with a bottle and stabbed me, resulting in about 20 stitches. When I went to the doctor, I'll never forget her words: she said if I had arrived just five minutes later, I would have been a dead woman due to the severity of my bleeding. That experience was a wake-up call for me, and it was more than enough reason to wholeheartedly say yes to God.

I found myself in a situation where I was sleeping with my enemy. The devil knew that I had made up my mind to start serving God, so he tried to use the very thing that I loved to try and take me out. But because my commitment to God was genuine, He intervened and saved me from the clutches of death. I share this to emphasize the importance of letting go and letting God.

Running out of an abusive relationship is essential. Living with a man for 11 years, having babies, and taking care of household chores does not make you a wife. From the moment you had that first baby out of wedlock, if he truly wanted to marry you, he would have done so.

You did everything in your power to please him, giving him everything that a husband should receive, yet he still didn't marry you. You see, there's no excitement left in such situations. Half the time, these men will meet someone else who presents them with a challenge and quickly make her a wife, while you've been tirelessly trying to make him happy.

Unbeknownst to you, you were giving a boyfriend what only a husband should receive. I can relate because I used to do the same before I got saved, and it yielded no benefit.

Chapter 15

The Nightmare of My Past

I remember nights when I could not sleep unless I had something to smoke or drink. Witnessing my mother's struggles in her marriage filled me with hurt and pain, leading me to seek love in all the wrong places. My journey took a drastic turn when I became pregnant with my son. His father, when he found out I was pregnant, gave me a dark substance in a bottle, telling me I must drink it. However, a strong presence dropped in my spirit to share the bottle with my mother. She immediately rebuked the poison and said this baby will be born and be in good health and I threw the dark substance away. If I had drank what was in the bottle, both my son Maurice and I would have died. Little did I know, I was sleeping with the enemy—an individual seeking pleasure without the responsibilities that come with it. Thank God my son is now married and serves with me in ministry as a Minister.

This cycle persisted when I later met the father of my daughter, sending me into another nightmare. It was painful and I cried daily but even thou I didn't know God then he kept me. I was born to serve God, and He shielded me from so many dangers. One day I took the bus to Kingston. The bus driver stopped to pick up passengers and armed gunmen boarded the bus and held everyone at gunpoint. Miraculously, I emerged unharmed, the only passenger spared from robbery. Though the situation haunted me in my nightmares for days, I am eternally grateful for God's protection amidst danger.

After parting ways with my son's father, I found myself in relationships that nearly cost me my life. If you ever find yourself in a situation where your partner threatens your life, take my advice: run for safety. I experienced a brutal attack, enduring blows to my head with a bottle and being stabbed in my chest. When I was rushed to the doctor, she let me know that if I had arrived just five minutes later, I might not have survived. These past experiences served as reminders of the consequences of my poor choices.

As the black sheep in my family, I always had to fight for what I wanted. Despite the challenges, I refused to let my past dictate my future. I pursued my goals relentlessly, even going back to school to study cosmetology. But I didn't stop there—I opened my own salon at that time. Through it all, I learned that our experiences do not have to define our destiny. Friends may come and go, and seasons may change, but it is crucial to discern which relationships are worth developing.

I made the decision to distance myself from friends involved in witchcraft, recognizing the dangers of becoming entangled in the yoke of bondage. It is important to surround yourself with the right people who uplift and support you on your journey.

Chapter 16

Until I Say Yes to God,
I Never Experienced True Love

As for those home wreckers, the women who only date married men because they believe that married men provide better care for them. In the past, I found myself involved with a married man. One afternoon, while my mother and I were having lunch at a restaurant, he arrived at the same place for lunch. Before entering the restaurant, I noticed he had removed his wedding band. I approached him and questioned why he had done so. He explained that he assumed the lady I was dining with was my mother, and he didn't want her to know he was married. I confronted him, stating that regardless of appearances, he was indeed married, so removing his wedding band was deceptive. I was deeply unsettled by his actions, and right then and there, I made the decision to end our association. Despite the material comforts he provided, I refused to tolerate deceit, and I swiftly ended any ties with him.

During that time and all the drama, I was young and deep in the world. Dating a married person brings about a unique kind of emotional stress, especially during holidays when the man and his family are enjoying themselves, while you, as the side chick, are kept in the shadows, hidden from his wife under false pretenses like going to the barber or visiting his mother just to see you. It's time to remove yourself from such an adulterous relationship because even if he were to leave his wife, he would likely repeat the pattern with another woman, never truly considering you for marriage due to your past involvement in his deceitful schemes. Don't sell yourself short for a few dollars; while the married man may provide material comforts like a house, car, or even open a business for you, it's time to release him back to his wife. You never know if his wife is a praying woman, and you're treading on perilous ground. Remember, what goes around, comes around; escape the curse of such a relationship.

Married women can also engage in scheming behaviors. For those who have good husbands willing to give them the world, it's time to sever ties with bosses or coworkers with whom you're having affairs, often resorting to lies to cover your tracks. Neglecting your husband, keeping the house in disarray, and failing to prepare meals are signs of a troubled heart that must be addressed.

If you break up someone's happy home, don't expect yours to be happy. Dealing with my relationship program, Matters of The Heart has taught me valuable lessons about relationships. Some individuals find it challenging to move on due to past hurts or feelings for ex-partners, even when they've entered new relationships. Witnessing an ex with someone else can trigger feelings of jealousy and even violence.

Sexual unions outside of God's ordained institution of marriage can form unholy covenants orchestrated by

Satan. While God unites husbands and wives in holy matrimony, Satan attempts to imitate this divine union by binding individuals in ungodly covenants.

Did you know that whoever you engage in sexual intercourse with becomes intertwined with your soul? That person becomes intricately connected to you, along with everyone they have been intimate with before. Consequently, you may be carrying the essence of numerous individuals whom you have never met or interacted with directly. By engaging with a prostitute or a harlot, you become linked to their souls, which can lead to feelings of being lost, alone, and depressed.

Vows, commitments, and agreements also play a significant role in forming soul ties. Vows have the power to bind the soul, as mentioned in Numbers 30:2. Marriage itself is built upon vows and binds two individuals together, as stated in Ephesians 5:31. Therefore, it is essential not to overlook the impact of vows and commitments in creating soul ties.

To embrace authentic love, you must release all

bitterness and hurt from past relationships. Through my journey as a Christian, I have learned that experiencing genuine love starts with falling in love with Jesus. By embracing the person God created you to be and loving yourself for who you are, you open yourself up to love others authentically. When you have encountered the true love of God, you refuse to settle for anything less because you recognize your worth in Him. Don't lower your standards for someone who is not ordained by God to be a part of your destiny.

Chapter 17

Not Every Friend Can Be Trusted In Your Personal Business

Growing up, the source of my mother's greatest pain was her best friend, despite my father being the one at fault. My father carried on a relationship with my mother's best friend, and he was shamelessly deceitful about it. He even went as far as opening a bar for his sweetheart, who happened to be my mother's friend. After finishing work, his first stop would always be at her place, where he would spend hours with his friends. From our home, we could see my father's vehicle parked in her yard after 5 PM, sometimes not returning home until midnight. My mother, who raised chickens on our farm, would unknowingly provide him with chicken, believing he would sell them and give her the money on weekends. Little did she know, he was giving them to his sweetheart for free. I witnessed a lot during my childhood.

Despite the mistreatment, my mother, being the Christian woman she was, would ensure his dinner was ready when he arrived home late. I vividly remember the hurt my mother endured as my father lavished his sweetheart's children with expensive private schooling while my sister and I attended government schools. Many nights, I saw my mother sitting and crying because of my father's mistreatment, all due to her best friend's betrayal.

Ladies, never disclose your personal life too freely to a best friend, as some friends harbor jealousy and are instruments of the devil sent to bring you down. I believe jealousy played a significant role in my mother's friend's betrayal. Despite my father's infidelity, he would still bring home flowers for my mother every day. My mother was a hardworking woman who ran her own business and was thriving, so it's likely her friend knew a lot about her personal affairs, which ultimately led to her betrayal.

This experience was bittersweet growing up. When a man cheats, the first place it affects is his home because his actions are not aligned with his words. As the Bible states in Matthew 6:24, "No one can serve two masters. Either you will hate the one and love the other, or you will be devoted to the one and despise the other."

So, whoever captures that love, that's who gets their time, but they still want to have you as the wife or husband in their corner. It cannot work like that; you have to know your worth. My mom migrated to the United States and got a divorce from my dad. At the time, I couldn't say anything because I knew the hell she had been through with him. Your peace is everything; sometimes, you might have to make decisions beyond your control, but it will work out for your good. Living your life in pain, hurt, and misery will only ruin your life. You have to choose wisely and make wise decisions. I always tell the single people I counsel about relationships that if they are saved, that means their spouse should be saved too.

As 2 Corinthians 6:14-16 says: "Don't be unequally yoked with unbelievers, for what fellowship do righteousness and iniquity have? Or what fellowship does light have with darkness?"

When you are unequally yoked, that's where the problem lies. You're going to church on a Sunday, and your spouse decides to go to the bar until you come from church—that's a red flag, and you need to be mindful of the warning signs. Marriage doesn't change anybody; God does.

Chapter 18

How Did the Life I Saw My Mom Live Affect Mine?

I was very angry and bitter to see the hurt and pain my mother had been through and still had to be that submitted wife to her husband. I couldn't understand why at the time until I was much older and started dating. Then I realized that I became angry and bitter in my relationships because I was afraid of going through what I saw my mother go through. So, I had a guard up even against friends, and I had trust issues going on. This memory and torment really disappeared when I got saved. Before that, I was living a life of nightmares, wondering if I would go through the same thing I saw my mom go through.

Now, since I got saved, I understand the bitter heart kind of situation. Bitterness is unresolved, unforgiven anger and resentment. It is the result of anger changing from an experience to a belief. Bitterness is seething and constant. Bitter people carry the same burdens as angry people, but to a greater extent. Watch out that no bitter root of unbelief rises up among you, for whenever it springs up, many are corrupted by its poison. (Hebrews 12:15, NLT)

Bitterness is a poison that can contaminate your whole life and even those close to you.

Do you want the cure for bitterness? You must understand that the only cure for bitterness and anger is forgiveness.

Bitterness is focused on what has been done to you. To break up bitterness, you must also be willing to look at what you have done to others.

Your task is to admit what your responsibility is in the matter and go to those you have hurt, confess your sin, and first seek their forgiveness. You must be willing to get the speck out of your own eye before you examine your neighbor's eye. That's where a lot of people go wrong; we tend to judge others but never see what's standing before us. It's important to clear your part.

(Matthew 7:3-5) "And why worry about a speck in your friend's eye when you have a log in your own? How can you think of saying, 'Let me help you get rid of that speck in your eye,' when you can't see past the log in your own eye? Hypocrite! First, get rid of the log from your own eye; then perhaps you will see well enough to deal with the speck in your friend's eye."

The examination process begins with you. Start with yourself and seek God's help in revealing the contents of your heart in relation to how you have sinned against others.

"Search me, O God, and know my heart; test me and know my thoughts. Point out anything in me that offends you, and lead me along the path of everlasting life." (Psalm 139:23-24, NLT)

The life my mother endured, marked by pain and

submission, left a profound impact on my own journey. Witnessing her silent suffering and steadfast commitment to her marriage stirred within me a mixture of anger and bitterness. As I matured and entered into relationships of my own, I found myself guarded and distrustful, haunted by the fear of replicating her experiences. Yet, salvation brought clarity and healing to my tormented soul, dispelling the shadows of my past and illuminating a path towards forgiveness and freedom.

Bitterness, I learned, is a poison that corrodes the soul, festering in the depths of unresolved anger and resentment. Hebrews 12:15 warns of the dangers of harboring bitterness, likening it to a destructive root that corrupts not only the individual but also those in their midst. The antidote to bitterness, I discovered, lies in forgiveness – a transformative act that releases the captive heart from the chains of resentment and grants liberation.

Acknowledging my own faults and seeking forgiveness from those I have wronged became essential steps on the journey to healing. Matthew 7:3-5 emphasizes the importance of self-examination and humility, urging individuals to confront their own shortcomings before attempting to judge others. Through sincere repentance and introspection, I began to untangle the knots of bitterness that had ensnared my heart, allowing God to illuminate the depths of my soul and guide me on the path to restoration.

Drawing inspiration from the story of Hannah in 1 Samuel, I realized the power of prayer in overcoming barrenness and despair. Like Hannah, I brought my struggles before God, pouring out my heart in earnest supplication. Despite the barrenness of my circumstances, prayer became a lifeline, bridging the gap between despair and hope. Through unwavering faith and commitment, I witnessed the transformative power of prayer as God opened doors and brought forth blessings in unexpected ways.

While the echoes of my mother's pain once overshadowed my life and relationships, salvation provided a beacon of hope amidst the darkness. Though adversity threatened to derail my dreams and aspirations, I persevered, determined to carve out a future defined by faith, resilience, and unwavering trust in God's promises.

Despite the hardships and heartbreaks along the way, I emerged stronger and more resilient, empowered by the knowledge that God's grace is sufficient to overcome every obstacle.

Only God can deliver you from the pain of your past. A lot of people are not delivered because they are trying to deliver themselves, but only God can deliver you. In 1 Samuel 1, the Bible talks about Hannah being unable to conceive a child. Hannah knew her husband loved her, but even his encouragement could not comfort her. She could not keep from hearing Peninnah's jeers and letting her hurtful words affect her self-confidence. Although we cannot prevent others from criticizing us, we can choose how we react to their words. Instead of dwelling on our problems, we can enjoy the loving relationships that God has given us.

Hannah had good reason to feel discouraged and bitter. She was unable to bear children, and she also shared her husband with another woman (1 Samuel 1:7). Her husband could not solve her problem, but instead of reacting in anger or giving up hope, she brought her problem honestly before God. We may face times of barrenness, embarrassment, even shame and disgrace when nothing seems to be happening in our work, service, or relationships. Praying in faith is difficult when we feel ineffective and alone. But as Hannah discovered, prayer opens the way for God to work (1 Samuel 1:19-20). Whatever is going on in your life, prayers can break through every barrier.

Hannah made a vow to God in prayer that if she were able to conceive a son, she would dedicate him back to God. Eventually, God heard her prayer and blessed her with a son, whom she dedicated back to God as she had promised.

Witnessing what my mom went through in her marriage used to deeply affect my life and relationships. It was as if I began to internalize her pain, seeking love in all the wrong places and dating the wrong people. Every time something went awry in my life, I couldn't help but recall the hurt and pain my mom endured. I even had to date someone to finish my schooling while my dad was preoccupied with his sweetheart and their children. Watching them go to private school while my sister and I attended public school was a constant reminder of the brokenness in our home.

The turmoil of a broken home made it difficult for me to focus in school. Sometimes, I'd sit in class worrying about my mom, and this affected my academic performance, causing me to fall behind. However, despite these challenges, I persevered. After completing my exams and graduating, I immediately sought employment and rented an apartment to distance myself from the pressure at home. Though I faced heartbreak and setbacks in relationships, I remained resilient. I continued working and pursued further education. It wasn't easy, but I refused to let adversity define me, and I eventually succeeded.

Chapter 19

Persecution In the Church

When I became a Christian and joined the church, I expected it to be a safe haven, but it turned out to be a place where I witnessed jealousy, gossip, and slander more than anywhere else. People seemed quicker to spread rumors and lies about me than to pray for me. I faced rejection from certain members of the congregation because of my nationality. When I got married, rumors circulated that it was only for papers.

I vividly recall an incident where a minister came to my house to confront me aggressively because I didn't comply with her demands. She invaded my personal space, pointing her finger in my face, and I had to quickly retreat to my car to avoid confrontation. Shockingly, the pastor sided with her because of her high status in the church and her significant financial contributions. Furthermore, I noticed a pattern where the pastor would turn the congregation against anyone who left the church. Those who departed were ostracized, labeled as witches, and persecuted.

Despite these challenges, I remained steadfast in my faith, knowing that God had not forsaken me.

I remember one afternoon, after serving as an usher, I went to retrieve my handbag and Bible, only to find graveyard dirt scattered all over my belongings. When I brought this to the pastor's attention, he confirmed what it was. It saddened me deeply to see how the fear of God had seemingly departed from many people and churches. Despite my dedication to serving, I faced baseless accusations, such as being involved with the pastor or stealing church funds.

If it weren't for my love for God, I might have been tempted to return to my old ways of drinking, partying, and smoking. Sometimes, it feels like certain churches are standing in the way of sinners. I'll never forget being labeled a witch simply because I wore a red scarf to a service. The preacher singled out anyone wearing a red scarf, insinuating they were witches and would face dire consequences. This hurt deeply, especially since my husband and I held the apostle in high regard.

All the persecution I endured served as preparation for our own ministry. Now, my husband and I lead our own ministry, despite facing criticism and opposition from some prophets and apostles who once prophesied about the work God would do through us in ministry. It's disheartening to see leaders who have forgotten their own humble beginnings and now judge others without knowing their relationship with God. We must be cautious not to judge others unfairly, as we never truly know their spiritual journey.

Many leaders become ensnared by titles, positions, large congregations, and the allure of glamour, failing to recognize that God is not found in such things. We must be focused on our Father's business, which is about winning souls. We need to be willing to go into the highways and byways, compelling people to come to God. Some individuals may never step foot in a church, so it's our responsibility to reach out to them wherever they are.

Chapter 20

God Don't Bless Mess

Many times, we find ourselves making our own choices and then trying to drag God into the mix, especially in relationships and marriages. But we must ask ourselves, did God truly sanction these connections, places, and decisions? Making plans without seeking God's guidance is akin to purchasing a ticket to an unknown destination. When you arrive at that place, you're at the mercy of whatever you encounter because you failed to conduct proper due diligence. In our Christian journey, it's imperative to seek God's counsel in every aspect of our lives.

Acts 17:28 reminds us, "For in him we live, and move, and have our being." This underscores the necessity of seeking God in all our actions and decisions. While some may seek quick prophetic words for guidance, it's crucial to remember that even if such a word is received, it still requires seeking God for its manifestation. I've made numerous wrong decisions in the past due to a lack of guidance when I was new to my faith. Therefore, it's essential to make wise decisions and allow God to lead us in all things.

Chapter 21

Never Let What People Say About You Keep You Defeated

When you allow others to define your identity, you end up living out their perceptions instead of embracing who God says you are. It's crucial to understand your true identity and strive to become the best version of yourself. Despite all the trials I've faced, I've remained steadfast in my commitment to glorify God in every aspect of my life. It's essential to have a clear vision and diligently work towards its fulfillment. When you're guided by a vision and a divine assignment, it provides the motivation needed to keep moving forward. Additionally, surrounding yourself with the right people is crucial. When God is preparing to bless you, He will connect you with individuals who will support and uplift you along the way.

About The Author

Prophetess Dr. Lovan Sands is supported in her ministry by her son, who serves as her assistant Pastor. Her daughter is presently completing her education in Jamaica. Originally from Jamaica, Prophetess Sands now resides in the Bahamas, where she has enjoyed 12 fruitful years of marriage to Apostle Elvin Sands. Together, they pastor Chosen Vessels International, a ministry they have led for 5 impactful years. With over 16 years of unwavering commitment to Christ, Prophetess Sands holds certifications as a Life Coach, Christian Counselor, and a certified Prison Chaplain, all earned from the esteemed Heart Bible Institute University.

Driven by her thirst for knowledge and spiritual growth, Prophetess Sands has pursued further education from various universities. She obtained her Doctor of Divinity degree from the Heart Bible Institute University and completed her Associates Degree in Biblical Studies at North Carolina Theological Seminary. Additionally, she is a Certified Mental Health Coach from the Heart Bible Institute

University and holds certification as a cosmetologist from the National Vocational College in Jamaica. As a dynamic preacher, teacher, and prophetic vessel, she demonstrates profound proficiency in the prophetic ministry and is highly effective in deliverance.

Countless lives have been transformed through Prophetess Sands' ministry, as she remains dedicated to seeking the heart of God. Her guiding motto is rooted in Hebrews 11:6 - "Without faith, it is impossible to please God."

Prophetess Sands also extends her ministry through digital platforms.

"Matters of the Heart," a relationship focused platform
Facebook.com/DrLovanSands,
Live sessions every Tuesday at 7:00 PM EST.

"Morning Inspirations"
Facebook.com/ChoosenVesselsIntl,
Monday - Friday at 6:00 AM EST.

PERSECUTED
BUT NOT
FORSAKEN

JOURNAL

Persecuted But Not Forsaken Notes: _____

_____

_____

_____

_____

_____

_____

_____

_____

_____

_____

_____

_____

_____

_____

_____

_____

_____

_____

_____

_____

_____

Persecuted But Not Forsaken Notes: _____

_____

_____

_____

_____

_____

_____

_____

_____

_____

_____

_____

_____

_____

_____

_____

_____

_____

_____

_____

_____

_____

_____

_____

Persecuted But Not Forsaken Notes: _____

Persecuted But Not Forsaken Notes: _____

Persecuted But Not Forsaken Notes: _____

_____

_____

_____

_____

_____

_____

_____

_____

_____

_____

_____

_____

_____

_____

_____

_____

_____

_____

_____

_____

_____

_____

Persecuted But Not Forsaken Notes: _____

Persecuted But Not Forsaken Notes: _____

_____

_____

_____

_____

_____

_____

_____

_____

_____

_____

_____

_____

_____

_____

_____

_____

_____

_____

_____

_____

_____

_____

_____

Persecuted But Not Forsaken Notes: _____

_____

_____

_____

_____

_____

_____

_____

_____

_____

_____

_____

_____

_____

_____

_____

_____

_____

_____

_____

_____

_____

_____

_____

_____

Persecuted But Not Forsaken Notes: _____

_____

_____

_____

_____

_____

_____

_____

_____

_____

_____

_____

_____

_____

_____

_____

_____

_____

_____

_____

_____

_____

_____

_____

Persecuted But Not Forsaken Notes: _____

_____

_____

_____

_____

_____

_____

_____

_____

_____

_____

_____

_____

_____

_____

_____

_____

_____

_____

_____

_____

_____

_____

_____

Persecuted But Not Forsaken Notes: _____

_____

_____

_____

_____

_____

_____

_____

_____

_____

_____

_____

_____

_____

_____

_____

_____

_____

_____

_____

_____

_____

_____

Persecuted But Not Forsaken Notes: _____

_____

_____

_____

_____

_____

_____

_____

_____

_____

_____

_____

_____

_____

_____

_____

_____

_____

_____

_____

_____

_____

_____

Persecuted But Not Forsaken Notes: _____

_____

_____

_____

_____

_____

_____

_____

_____

_____

_____

_____

_____

_____

_____

_____

_____

_____

_____

_____

_____

_____

Persecuted But Not Forsaken Notes: _____

_____

_____

_____

_____

_____

_____

_____

_____

_____

_____

_____

_____

_____

_____

_____

_____

_____

_____

_____

_____

_____

_____

Persecuted But Not Forsaken Notes: _____

_____

_____

_____

_____

_____

_____

_____

_____

_____

_____

_____

_____

_____

_____

_____

_____

_____

_____

_____

_____

_____

_____

_____

Persecuted But Not Forsaken Notes: _____

_____

_____

_____

_____

_____

_____

_____

_____

_____

_____

_____

_____

_____

_____

_____

_____

_____

_____

_____

_____

_____

_____

_____

_____

_____

_____

Persecuted But Not Forsaken Notes: _____

_____

_____

_____

_____

_____

_____

_____

_____

_____

_____

_____

_____

_____

_____

_____

_____

_____

_____

_____

Persecuted But Not Forsaken Notes: _____

_____

_____

_____

_____

_____

_____

_____

_____

_____

_____

_____

_____

_____

_____

_____

_____

_____

_____

_____

_____

_____

_____

_____

Persecuted But Not Forsaken Notes: _____

_____

_____

_____

_____

_____

_____

_____

_____

_____

_____

_____

_____

_____

_____

_____

_____

_____

_____

_____

_____

Persecuted But Not Forsaken Notes: _____

_____

_____

_____

_____

_____

_____

_____

_____

_____

_____

_____

_____

_____

_____

_____

_____

_____

_____

_____

_____

_____

_____

www.ingramcontent.com/pod-product-compliance
Lightning Source LLC
Chambersburg PA
CBHW071019120626
46546CB00003B/1161